SAVE
THIS
SHIRT

Hannah Rogge
Photographs By
Adrian Buckmaster

STC CRAFT | A MELANIE FALICK BOOK
STEWART, TABORI & CHANG | NEW YORK

For Kevin Lertkhachonsuk
Because of your overwhelming
support, your great inspirational
finds, and the open door to your
house (with valuable table
space and a muse named Luna),
this is for you.

Published in 2007 by Stewart, Tabori & Chang
An imprint of Harry N. Abrams, Inc.

Photographs copyright © 2007 by
Adrian Buckmaster/Text and illustrations
copyright © 2007 by Hannah Rogge

Library of Congress Cataloging-in-Publication Data:
Rogge, Hannah.
Save this shirt / Hannah Rogge ; photographs by
Adrian Buckmaster. -- 1st ed.
p. cm.
"A Melanie Falick Book."
ISBN-13: 978-1-58479-584-1
ISBN-10: 1-58479-584-0
1. T-shirts. 2. Clothing and dress--Alteration.
3. Clothing and dress--Remaking. I. Title.
TT675.R64 2007
746--dc22
2006028842

Editor: Melanie Falick
Designer: Sarah Von Dreele
Production Manager: Anet Sirna-Bruder

The text of this book was composed in
Helvetica Neue, Cooper Black, and Washout.

Printed and bound in China
10 9 8 7 6 5 4 3 2 1

HNA ▌▌▌▌▌
harry n. abrams, inc.
a subsidiary of La Martinière Groupe

115 West 18th Street
New York, NY 10011
www.hnabooks.com

CONTENTS

◗ This project is a super-easy way to use up all those extra
bits and pieces — don't let the scraps go to waste!

This book is about transforming the large, shapeless, frumpy-looking T-shirts we all inevitably collect into useful and appealing wardrobe pieces and accessories. In other words, this book is about saving those shirts.

Like most everyone I know, I have piles of old T-shirts—leftovers from old boyfriends, charity-event giveaways, rock-concert souvenirs, gifts from relatives' travels, the list goes on and on. And for some reason, I'm reluctant to get rid of them. Yeah, they're comfortable—cotton jersey is pretty cozy—and some of them have nostalgic value, but let's face it: There are only so many shirts a girl can sleep in or take to the gym and, besides, most of the time these shirts aren't even flattering.

I work for a design firm, and part of my job entails building Christmas window displays for department stores in Manhattan—the complex kind that tourists line up to see every year. Inevitably, television crews show up while we're working, so my bosses have learned to take advantage of the advertising potential of the situation by issuing all of the employees T-shirts with the company logo emblazoned on them. Size options are large and larger, and wearing the shirts is mandatory. The first year this happened, not only did the cameras catch me looking like a sack in this gargantuan top, but the darn shirt kept getting caught on my knees, making it hard for me to move around and do my job. That's when I got the idea to deconstruct and refashion oversized T-shirts and to flaunt my own style, creativity, and craftiness. As long as I'm advertising for the company, why not advertise for myself a little bit, right?

There are lots of things to make with a T-shirt. In this book I have included my favorite ideas. I love figuring out how to take something ordinary and translate it into something special, particularly when I can do it for almost no money. I hope the projects I offer in this book, along with the jumpstart of the shirt included, inspire you to **save this shirt, too.**

BEFORE YOU START

You should know that "saving" these shirts is very easy.

You really don't need a whole lot of skill in fashion, sewing, or even cutting fabric. There are, however, a few pointers you should keep in mind as you begin.

Not All T-Shirts Are Created Equal

T-shirts vary in size, weight, shape, condition, and decorative elements, so it's always a good idea to assess the shirt and the project you have in mind for it before you start. Ask yourself questions like: Is the fabric thick or thin, and how does it drape? If there is a stain, will it still be part of the new shirt or will you cut it out? If there is a logo, where will it end up? Try to use as much of the shirt as possible; if there are scraps left over from one project, you can often use them to make another one.

T-Shirts Can Shrink

T-shirts are generally made of 100% cotton or a cotton-polyester blend. Even if the tag says it's preshrunk, if the T-shirt is new (or close to new) wash it before you start to ensure it will not change size after you have restyled it.

Mark Carefully

Most of the instructions in this book involve marking lines on the shirts while they are on your work surface. I recommend using a piece of tailor's chalk, pins (straight ones when marking a garment that's not on you; safety pins when making adjustments while wearing a shirt), or pencils so that after you iron or wash the finished piece, the marks are no longer visible. Before you make any irreversible cuts, however, you might want to try the shirt on and make any final refinements while looking in the mirror. And always remember that it is the stitches from seam to seam that will define the size of the finished piece, not the cut line.

Pins Help

Use straight pins to hold two pieces of fabric together as you sew. Be sure to align the pins so that both pieces of fabric stay smooth.

Cut Slowly

One of the great things about T-shirt fabric—it's called jersey, if you want to get technical—is that the edges do not fray when cut. This is extremely handy when cutting necklines, sleeves, and hems. Cut (or ripped) edges—sometimes referred to as raw edges—don't necessarily need to be hemmed and can become a design element instead.

If you're planning on raw edges, however, you do need to watch that you cut carefully so you don't end up with jags in the fabric. This happens when the fabric wiggles while you're working or when it wrinkles under the scissors' blade. Keep the shirt flat on a surface and cut slowy. If you are having difficulty, cut one piece at a time (if the instructions tell you to cut both pieces together, you can cut the top piece first, and then the bottom piece along the same line). Also try holding the fabric slightly taut with one hand while you cut with the other hand.

The Iron Is Your Friend

Some T-shirts lie flatter than others, depending on how they were made (for example, if the seams weren't sewn straight, the fabric is likely to skew) and how they have been treated since then. For reconstructing and restyling, the flatter a shirt lies the better, so ironing is often a key step. If you are using a portion of the shirt, then only iron what you need. Ironing is also helpful when you want to hold folded fabric in place.

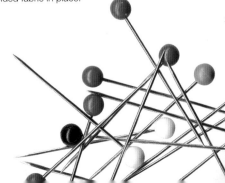

You Can Stitch by Hand or by Machine

I find standard sewing machines intimidating but, thanks to my friend Vanessa, I have learned to use a miniature sewing machine and really enjoy it. It fits in my apartment and only does one kind of stitch, the running stitch, which is all I need. I used both the mini machine and the tried-and-true needle and thread for all of the projects in this book. When my friend Cindy stepped in to test the project instructions, she had no interest in hand-sewing and did everything on a standard machine. I tell you this because it shows that you can complete all of the projects in this book by hand or with a mini or standard-size sewing machine. I've included here three different types of stitches you can use: the practical running stitch and the more decorative cross and whip stitches. Just remember: When you are hand-sewing, knot your thread at the end of each seam so your stitches will stay put; when machine-sewing, stitch forward and then backward about an inch at the beginning and end of each seam.

Practice Makes Perfect

Although the goal of this book is to show you how easy it is to transform unflattering or unwearable T-shirts into wearable shirts and accessories you love, you probably don't want to start with a shirt you treasure. If you suspect that your skills are not up to your personal standards, I suggest that you practice on a less-than-awesome shirt (perhaps one with a big stain). Once you've got the basics down, you can restyle the Save This Shirt T-shirt that came with this book or any other cool one you have in your stash.

RUNNING STITCH

All of the shirts in this book are made using a running stitch. This is the most basic stitch in both hand and machine sewing. The thread just passes in and out of the fabric, resulting in a straight line of stitches.

To add interest to the running stitch, you can vary the length of your stitches or the color of your thread, or you can use embroidery floss or yarn instead of thread—as long as you always keep in mind the purpose of the stitches. If you're sewing a side seam, you probably don't want to make stitches so long that the seam has holes in it or won't hold. And, of course, you need to match the thickness of your thread, floss, or yarn to the size of the hole in your needle.

For a decorative effect, you may want to use a whip or cross stitch. The whip stitch is good for creating an edge of bold color, while the cross stitch is good for incorporating a repeated pattern into the design. I like to use both whip and cross stitches over running stitch seams to help define them.

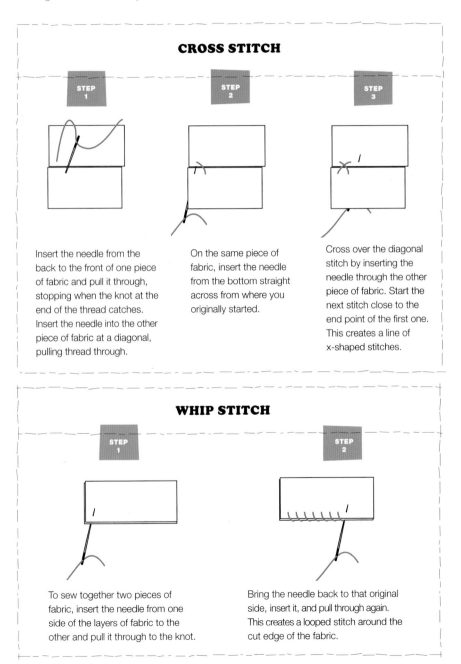

CROSS STITCH

STEP 1

Insert the needle from the back to the front of one piece of fabric and pull it through, stopping when the knot at the end of the thread catches. Insert the needle into the other piece of fabric at a diagonal, pulling thread through.

STEP 2

On the same piece of fabric, insert the needle from the bottom straight across from where you originally started.

STEP 3

Cross over the diagonal stitch by inserting the needle through the other piece of fabric. Start the next stitch close to the end point of the first one. This creates a line of x-shaped stitches.

WHIP STITCH

STEP 1

To sew together two pieces of fabric, insert the needle from one side of the layers of fabric to the other and pull it through to the knot.

STEP 2

Bring the needle back to that original side, insert it, and pull through again. This creates a looped stitch around the cut edge of the fabric.

The Winner

work kit

- ○ Oversized T-shirt for restyling (ironed, if desired)
- ○ Well-fitting T-shirt or other type of pullover to use as pattern guide
- ○ Iron (optional)
- ○ Tailor's chalk or pencil (for marking)
- ○ Straight pins
- ○ Scissors
- ○ Needle and thread

The Winner is custom-fitted, comfortable, and flattering. To make it, choose a well-fitting shirt from your wardrobe and use it as a pattern guide for restyling an oversized T-shirt. You can follow the pattern exactly or customize the neckline, sleeves, and length as desired.

STEP 1

Turn the oversized shirt inside out and place it flat on a work surface, with the front facing up.

STEP 2

Turn the well-fitting shirt inside out and lay it on top of the oversized shirt, front side up, so the necklines of the two shirts are as close to each other as possible. If the collars don't match up, make sure that the shirts are centered at the top and that the shoulder seams of each shirt touch.

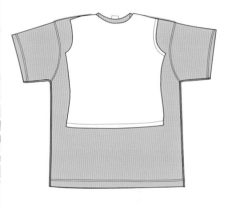

STEP 3

Using tailor's chalk or pencil and starting under the bottom of the sleeve and ending at the bottom of the well-fitting shirt, trace ½" out from the left side. (This is to allow room for stitching.) Pin together the front and back of the oversized shirt inside the line you have just traced.

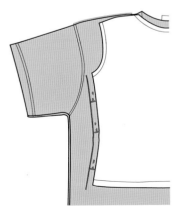

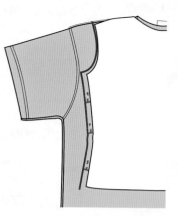

Mark where the sleeve of the well-fitting shirt ends by drawing a line on the oversized shirt. If you want a finished edge, leave ½" between the line and the edge of the shirt; if you are happy with a cut edge, do not leave any space. **NOTE:** *To change the style of the sleeves, see page 14.*

Repeat steps 3 and 4 for the right side of the shirt.

When you lay the fitted shirt on top of the one to adjust, it's likely that the fitted shirt's sleeves will be in between the sleeve seams of the shirt underneath. It is possible, however, that the sleeves of the shirt on top will overlap the arm seams of the shirt you want to fix. Marking and adjusting sleeves around an existing seam gets tricky, so I suggest you mark where the sleeves of the fitted shirt begin and then continue with the rest of the instructions. This way you can decide what to do with the sleeves after you have fixed the shirt's width.

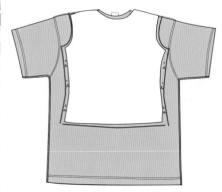

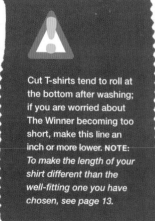

Cut T-shirts tend to roll at the bottom after washing; if you are worried about The Winner becoming too short, make this line an inch or more lower. NOTE: *To make the length of your shirt different than the well-fitting one you have chosen, see page 13.*

Using tailor's chalk or pencil, mark a line from side to side ½" from the bottom edge of the well-fitting shirt.

Set aside the well-fitting T-shirt.
Cut along the lines drawn on the
oversized shirt, cutting through
both front and back together.

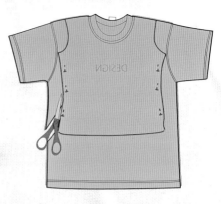

On the left side of the shirt,
sew the top and bottom pieces
together, starting under the sleeve
and ending at the bottom edge.
Repeat on the right side. Turn
the shirt right side out. **NOTE:** *For
decorative seam options, see
page 6.*

If desired, cut off the collar of the
shirt by cutting just outside of the
stitched seam that holds the collar
to the body of the shirt. **NOTE:** *For
other neckline options, see page 12.*

DESIGN

Variations on a Winning Theme

Use the variations shown here to dress up The Winner or any other T-shirt you're reconstructing.

NECKLINES

Use these for the front and/or back of your T-shirts.

Scoop Neck, V-neck, Square Neck

STEP 1
Put the shirt on. Mark the center of the original collar with tailor's chalk, pencil, or a pin. Then mark (also in the center) how low you would like the new neckline to go.

STEP 2
Take the shirt off. On one side, draw half of the neckline you want (scoop, V-, or square) from the shoulder seam to the mark you just made.

NOTE: *If you don't think you can make the perfect half of a neckline swoop, find a shirt in your wardrobe with a neckline you like. Position this shirt under the shirt you are refashioning so top of desired neckline is where you want to start neckline on new shirt. Press down on the new shirt to feel the outline of the good shirt's neckline. Trace this arc onto the new shirt.*

STEP 3
Cut along the drawn line from the shoulder to the center point of the neckline, making sure to cut only the top piece of fabric.

STEP 4
Fold the cut material and align it with the other side of the neck. Using the cut edge of this folded piece as a guide, cut the other side of the neck, again only cutting the top fabric.

STEP 5
Remove the back of the neck by cutting just outside the seam line of the original collar.

Ripped Neck

STEP 1
Put the shirt on and, with a pin pointing crosswise, mark how deep you want the center of the neckline to be.

STEP 2
Take the shirt off. Carefully snip about ½" at the center of shirt's front, making sure to cut through the collar.

STEP 3
Grab fabric on each side of the snip and slowly pull the pieces apart down center of shirt. Stop pulling when rip reaches pin mark.

LENGTH

Customize the length of your T-shirts according to your body type, the latest trend, or any other criteria you choose. You might even consider cutting the bottom of the T-shirt diagonally so that the shape is intentionally asymmetrical. By following the instructions for The Winner but extending the length as explained below, you can turn an oversized T-shirt into a flattering dress.

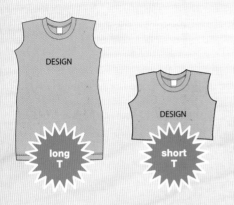

Long T or Short T

NOTE: *When choosing a shirt to restyle, keep in mind that the original length of your oversized shirt will determine the maximum length of your restyled T.*

STEP 1
Trace a well-fitting T-shirt onto your oversized T-shirt along the sides and sleeves as instructed for The Winner on page 9. Pin the front and back of the oversized shirt together, inside the mark you drew.

STEP 2
For a Long T, extend the bottom of the drawn line down to the bottom edge of the oversized shirt. For a Short T, draw a line from one side of the shirt to the other at the desired length.

STEP 3
Cut the oversized shirt along the lines drawn, cutting through both layers of fabric at once.

STEP 4
Sew up the sides from sleeves to bottom edge.

SLEEVES

The easiest way to restyle sleeves is simply to cut them off for that "rocker" look, but after a while that can get boring. So here are instructions for a few other variations.

Narrower Sleeves

NOTE: *This variation must be made before you have cut and sewn The Winner.*

STEP 1
Trace the pattern of the well-fitting shirt and then set it aside. Draw a line parallel to the top of the shirt's sleeve that extends from the edge of the armhole to the bottom of the drawn sleeve line.

STEP 2
Extra material at the armhole can make some sleeves tricky. To accommodate for this, draw a mark ½" above the bottom of the armhole. Connect this point to the end of the line you just drew.

STEP 3
Use this new diagonal line as your new guide line for the shirt sleeve. Cut out the shirt and sew together as directed for The Winner.

Shorter Sleeves

STEP 1
Put the shirt on. With tailor's chalk, pencil, or a pin, mark the desired length on one sleeve.

STEP 2
Take the shirt off and cut the sleeve as marked. If, in shortening the sleeve, you have cut through your sleeve seam, reinforce your stitches with a new sleeve seam.

STEP 3
Line up your scrap piece with the other sleeve and use as a cutting guide.

Tank Top

STEP 1
Cut off each sleeve, using the armhole seam as a guide. Try on the shirt. If the shoulder fabric still extends too far over your shoulder, mark the desired width on the top of one shoulder using tailor's chalk, pencil, or a pin.

STEP 2
Take the shirt off. Cut an arc from this shoulder mark to the bottom of the armhole.

STEP 3
Line up your scrap piece with the other sleeve and use as a cutting guide.

Racer-Back Sleeves

STEP 1

If you have one, put a racer-back bra or tank top on underneath the T-shirt to use as a guide (if you don't have one, don't worry, just put on your T-shirt).

STEP 2

On the top of one shoulder, mark the width of the new shoulder with tailor's chalk or pencil. Then, on your shoulder blade, mark how far in towards the center of your back you want the sleeve to go. (You can use the racer-back top that you are wearing as a guide or create an original line.) The cut lines will be different for the front and back of the shirt.

STEP 3

Draw a deep scoop on the shirt's back from the seam of the shoulder to the armhole, following your marks from the previous step.

STEP 4

On the front of the shirt, mark a shallow scoop from shoulder seam to bottom of armhole.

STEP 5

Take the shirt off and cut a new armhole along the lines you have drawn, making sure to cut the front fabric and back fabric separately. Repeat for the other armhole, using the cut sleeve as a pattern. Remember that more material will be cut from the back of the sleeve than from the front.

Boxy Tank

work kit

- ○ T-shirt for restyling
- ○ Scissors
- ○ Tailor's chalk, pencil, or pins (for marking)
- ○ Straight-edge ruler

This is the quickest, easiest way of restyling a shirt because it only requires cutting and tying—no sewing! This is what I did to all of my T-shirts in the '80s when the movie *Flashdance* popularized the style. The softer or thinner the cotton of your T-shirt, the more gracefully the Boxy Tank will drape. Wear it on its own or try layering it over a tank top or another shirt.

Cut off the hem of each sleeve, using the seam lines as a guide, then cut open the seam on each one. Set aside the two hem strips.

Cut off the sleeves, making sure to cut inside the shoulder seam. Using tailor's chalk, pencil, or pins, mark 2" in from the sleeve openings on each side.

Using the lowest point of the front neck as a center point, draw a shallow scoop from the shoulder mark to the center point and cut along that mark. Cut only the top layer of fabric.

Fold the cut piece at the center point, lining it up with the other side of the collar and shoulder. Use this piece as a guide for cutting the other side of the neck to match. Cut the fabric in the back to match the scoop of the neck in the front.

Starting at the bottom center of shirt back, draw a straight vertical line about 5" high. Using this as a center line, draw a perpendicular line about 10" long so that you have drawn a "T" with 5" on either side of the stem. Cut the back of the shirt along your "T" mark, being careful not to cut the front of the shirt.

Using one of the reserved hem strips from the sleeves, tie a square knot around one of the shoulders of the shirt. (To make a square knot, cross one end of a strip over another, wrap it around and pull it through the loop; pull tight and repeat.) Repeat with the second hem strip on the other side.

Put the shirt on. With your hands behind your back, grab the loose flaps that were created when you cut out the "T" shape. Tie these flaps together in a square knot, adjusting the fit of the shirt to your own waist.

STEP 1

Cut off each sleeve, using armhole seam as a guide.

SCARF

This is more of a fashion piece than a scarf for warmth. Personalize it by adjusting the length to suit you, adding fringe to the ends, adorning it with patches, buttons, or beads, or cutting the ends with pinking shears. It can also be tied as a belt around your waist.

STEP 2

Using tailor's chalk or pencil, measure and mark 2" above the bottom of the shirt's left armhole.

Draw a diagonal line from the mark you just made down to the bottom of the shirt's right armhole. Cut a small notch at the end of this line, cutting through both layers of fabric. (This will serve as a guide later when you turn the shirt over.)

Measure 4" down from the line you just drew. Using tailor's chalk or a pencil and a ruler, draw a second line parallel to the first diagonal line. Cut a similar notch through both layers of fabric at each end of this line. Repeat to make a third line.

On the side that you started with (front left side), mark 4" beneath the lowest line. Make a notch at this mark.

Turn the shirt over. Skipping the uppermost mark on the front left side, draw lines connecting the notches to one another so that you have three more parallel lines. (In order to form one long strip of fabric, the diagonal lines on back should slant in same direction as lines on front.)

Cut along the diagonal line as marked, starting from the uppermost mark above left armhole and moving around the shirt from front to back, to create one long 4"-wide strip. Be sure to cut through only one piece of fabric (only the front or back) at a time. For a decorative effect, use pinking shears if desired. Wrap the scarf around your neck and cut to the desired length.

To make fringe, make 4" deep cuts every ½" at both ends of the scarf, and tie a knot at the end of each resulting strip. If desired, before tying the knot, slide a bead onto each strip or sew on decorative buttons.

T-Skirt

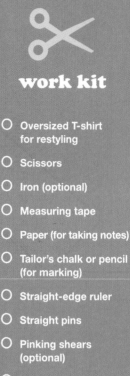

work kit

- Oversized T-shirt for restyling
- Scissors
- Iron (optional)
- Measuring tape
- Paper (for taking notes)
- Tailor's chalk or pencil (for marking)
- Straight-edge ruler
- Straight pins
- Pinking shears (optional)
- Needle and thread in matching or contrasting color

The T-Skirt is made by turning a T-shirt on its side, so that its width becomes the skirt's length. When choosing a shirt, consider whether it is wide enough to accommodate the length you desire and, if there is a graphic, consider if you're going to like the way it looks sideways (traveling vertically up your body). After you have made the skirt, you can adjust its length by cutting it shorter or sewing more T-shirt fabric around the hem for a slightly different, longer style.

CAMP
SUPERFUN!

Cut off the hem from the bottom of the shirt, using the hemline as a guide and cutting through both layers of fabric at once. Cut resulting loop once to create a long "hemmed" strip. Set this piece aside.

Turn the shirt inside out. Smooth or iron it as flat as possible, and position it on a work surface horizontally (so that a side seam and sleeve are facing you).

With the measuring tape, measure around your hips at the point where you would like the top of your skirt to sit. Divide that number in half (because you will be cutting front and back of the skirt together), and then add 1" (for seam allowance). Write this measurement on a piece of paper and label it "Top." Add 8" to this measurement. Write down this number and label it "Bottom."

$$30 \div 2 = 15$$
$$15 + 1 = 16$$
top 16"
+8
24" bottom

Starting under the shoulder and close to the side seam (but beyond any sleeve shaping), mark a line the length of your "Bottom" measurement with a ruler, paying attention to where any graphics on the T-shirt will fall on the skirt. Mark the beginning, center, and end of the line you have just drawn using tailor's chalk, pencil, or pins.

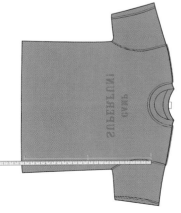

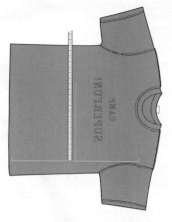

Make a 14" line perpendicular to the center point; the top of this is the center of the skirt Top.

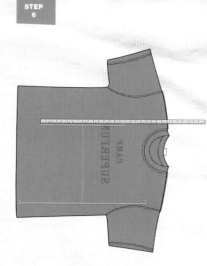

Mark a line the length of your Top measurement, maintaining the center point. Make sure the Top line is parallel to the Bottom line.

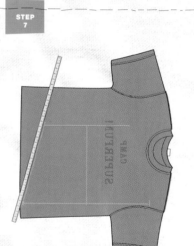

Draw a diagonal line from the left end of the Top measurement to the left end of the Bottom measurement. (You only have to mark one side.)

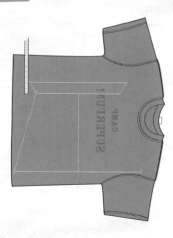

Measure and mark a line 2" above the Top line, extending this line out 1" on either side of the Top line. This is for the skirt's waistband. At each end, connect the Top line and the waistband line with short diagonal lines.

STEP 9

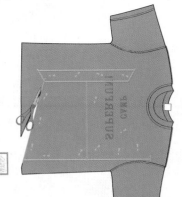

Pin the front and back together so they won't move when you cut the fabric. Begin cutting out the skirt on the diagonal, cutting both pieces of fabric together.

STEP 10

Cut the Bottom line across to the center mark. (If desired, use pinking shears for a decorative effect.) Cut the top of the waistband line to the center mark (again with pinking shears, if desired).

STEP 11

Fold the skirt in half at the marked center points. Using the cut side as a pattern, mark and cut out the second side.

STEP 12

Sew the front and back pieces of the skirt together along the long diagonal sides. Do not sew together the 2" waistband at the top. Turn the skirt right side out and position it so that the back of the skirt faces up.

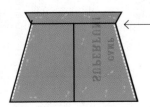

stop sewing here

Take the hemmed strip you cut earlier, fold it in half, and mark the center point. Place the strip, across the top of the skirt so that it touches the top of each diagonal, aligning the center of the strip with the center of the skirt.

Fold the waistband piece over the long strip and pin in place. Carefully sew the folded edge to the top layer of fabric, making sure that the strip underneath the fold remains free of your stitches.

Turn the skirt over so the front of the skirt faces you. In the center of the waistband, cut two holes 2" apart, just wide enough to fit the ends of the strip through (do not make these holes any wider than 1").

Bring each end of the strip around to the front and through a hole, so that when the top 2" of the waistband is folded over, the ends of the strip extend down the front of the skirt. Pin the folded piece down and sew it only to the top layer as you did for the back of the skirt, making sure to keep the strip away from your stitching line. Try skirt on and tie it in front. If the strip is too long, cut to desired length. To keep strip from falling out, tie knots at both ends.

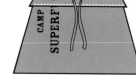

HEADBAND

I went to college with a guy named Jesse who kept his wild hair under control with the sleeve of a T-shirt. At the time I thought it was weird, but now I appreciate his ingenuity. You can scrunch up this headband for a '60s look, or smooth it out with the wider part of the sleeve toward the back of your head to make it look more like a head scarf. Or you can loop it around a ponytail like a more traditional hair scrunchie. If you want to get fancy, use pinking shears to cut the sleeve off the shirt, finish the edges by folding them and sewing them down, or embellish with embroidery or a small patch.

STEP 1

Cut one sleeve off shirt, using armhole seam as a guide.

STEP 2

For a wide headband, put what would be the armhole of the sleeve over your head. For a thinner headband, cut the part closest to the hemmed end to the width of your liking.

Arm-Bag

I am amused by silly things and in this case, it's the way you hold this bag—through the armholes of the original shirt. I also like that the finished bag is a clearly defined triangular shape. Depending on the original width of the shirt, the opening of this bag can end up being pretty wide. If you don't like the tie closure to this bag, it's very simple to sew in a zipper, as shown in the T-Bag instructions on page 51.

Fold the shirt in half, right side out, so the tops of the shoulders are aligned. Cut the neck at a diagonal so that both the front and back of the shirt have a V-neck. Start to cut just below the bottom of the hemmed neck, so that the original T-shirt neck is completely removed.

STEP
2

Cut off the hem from the bottom of the shirt, using the hemline as a guide and cutting through both layers of fabric at once. Cut resulting loop once to create a long, "hemmed" strip.

STEP
3

Cuff the bottom of the shirt up so there is a 1½" fold of fabric around the front and back of the shirt, and pin or iron in place. Make sure front and back of shirt are not pinned together.

STEP 4

Sew a line of stitches parallel to and 1¼" above the folded bottom, creating a tube around the bottom of the shirt. Make a small vertical cut in the tube to create an opening, being careful not to cut any stitches.

STEP 5

Attach a large safety pin or paper clip to one end of the hemmed strip and push it through the tube until it reaches the other side of the opening. Pin the two ends of the strip together so you don't lose the strip in the tube.

STEP 6

Cut the hemmed edges off both shirt sleeves. Cut each of these two small loops once to make two strips of fabric. Set aside.

STEP 7

Cut the rest of the sleeves off the shirt, cutting inside the original seam lines. If you want a thinner handle strap, cut deeper into the tops of the shoulders.

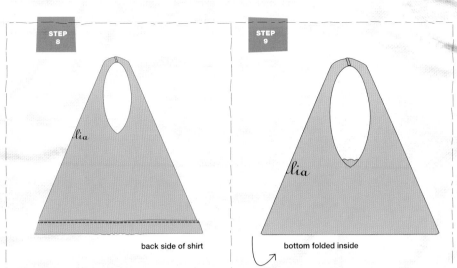

STEP 8

back side of shirt

STEP 9

bottom folded inside

Taking hold of front center of shirt in one hand and back center in other, pull pieces away from each other until shirt lies flat with tube at bottom. The original sides of the shirt are now at center of the bag, beneath the armholes, which are now unfolded.

Fold bottom of triangle up through the inside of shirt so the tube reaches the inside bottom of the armhole. Pin or iron the shirt into this position.

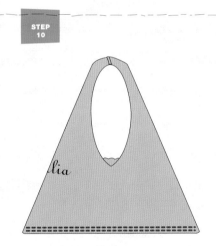

STEP 10

Sew two parallel lines of stitches along the bottom of the triangle.

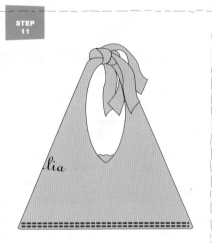

STEP 11

Use the small strips to tie the shoulders of the bag together (at top of triangle). On the inside of the bag, remove the pin that holds both ends of the strap together and tie the ends of the strip together to create a closure. **NOTE:** *If you prefer a zipper closure, follow instructions on page 51.*

Julie's Sailor T

work kit

- T-shirt for restyling
- Straight pins
- Tailor's chalk or pencil (for marking)
- Measuring tape
- Straight-edge ruler
- Scissors
- Needle and thread

I came up with this design by playing around with the idea of removing fabric from the front and back of a T-shirt rather than the sides. I had some trouble with the neckline until my good friend Julie, who is a master seamstress, suggested using a sailor's shirt as a model.

Put the shirt on right side out. Pinch shirt across each shoulder so the sleeve underarms fall at a comfortable place for you. Put a horizontal pin at the top of each shoulder to hold in place.

Take off the shirt and place it face down on a work surface. Using tailor's chalk or pencil, draw lines parallel to the T-shirt's shoulders at the height of the pins.

Pin across the lines just drawn. Pin the rest of the shirt so the top and bottom stay together.

Using a measuring tape, measure around your bust to determine how wide you want the shirt to be. Add ½" to this measurement and then divide that number by 4. (Fold the measuring tape into quarters if you don't want to do the math.)

Using the final number determined in step 4, measure and mark a line that distance in from each side of the shirt, so that you have two parallel lines running down the middle of the shirt.

Cut off each sleeve, using armhole seam as guide.

Cut off the top of the shoulders ¼" above the pinned line.

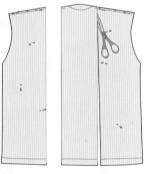

Carefully cut both the top and bottom fabrics along the vertical lines down the middle (use pinking shears for a decorative effect, if desired). You now have three separate pieces. Eliminate the middle piece.

Remove the pins that hold the top and bottom pieces in place, but keep the shoulder pins intact. Bring the left and right sides of ONLY the top layer together, pinning them so that the inside sides of the shirt touch and the outside sides face out, cut edges up. Flip the shirt over and repeat this step on the other side.

edges pinned together

side view

On the side of the T-shirt you want to be the front, sew the left and right pieces together about ¼" in from the cut edge, starting 10" (or desired length) down from the neck and continuing to the bottom.

Flip the shirt over. Sew together the back sides of the shirt as you did the front, starting 7" down from the neck and continuing to the bottom.

Unpin the shoulder lines. Turn the shirt inside out and put it on. Repin the shoulders where you determine they should be sewn. Fold the collar so it lays flat the way it will when it is right side out. Now determine how wide the neckline and shoulders should be, and mark width with pins. Using tailor's chalk or pencil, mark how far in from the shoulder the armholes should be by drawing a line from shoulder to underarm. (You can either mark both armholes now or use the scrap piece of one to determine the cut of the other one later.)

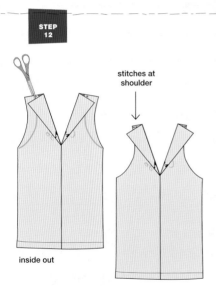

stitches at shoulder

inside out

Take the shirt off and cut the sleeves off, using your marked lines as a guide. Sew across the top of both shoulders.

right side out

Put the shirt on again. Adjust the collar to your liking by cutting it at the desired angle. If the arms do not fit as you like, pin and sew accordingly.

PATCHES

Method One
Sewing Patch onto Outside of T-shirt

STEP 1

Cut out graphic from the shirt to be saved, leaving about a ⅛" border around it. Pin the patch where you want it on the nicely fitted T-shirt. If the patch is really big, you may want to dab on some fabric glue to hold it in place as you sew.

STEP 2

Using a contrasting color of thread, sew all the way around the patch.

STEP 1

Cut out the graphic from the shirt to be saved, leaving ½" border around it. Decide where you would like to adhere the patch on the shirt that fits you. Cut a very small hole in the shirt at the center of that area.

STEP 2

Place patch underneath the shirt so that you can see the middle of it through the hole. Pin the patch into place.

STEP 3

Turn the shirt inside out and sew all around the edge of the patch. Make sure to knot your thread on the inside of the shirt.

STEP 4

Turn the shirt right side out again. Using the hole that you cut as a starting point, carefully cut out the material of the fitted shirt that overlaps the patch, staying about ⅛" away from the stitches.

Faux Hawk

This design is based on the mohawk hairdo. Tying the pieces together in the back makes them stick up a little bit while the rest of the shirt lies flat (just like the hairdo). If you prefer to keep the backside flat, you can sew the back pieces together instead of tying them.

Turn the shirt inside out. Cut off each sleeve, using the armhole seam as guide.

Fold the shirt in half to determine the center line on the front of the shirt. Mark with tailor's chalk or pencil.

Lay the shirt flat, front side up. Measure and mark two lines 3½" to the left and right of the center line. Each line should extend from the bottom of the shirt to the shoulders.

Pinch the fabric along the left side of the line so it stands 1" high. Pin the pinched fabric. To make this easier, if desired, iron the pinched fabric into position. Repeat on right side.

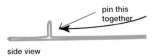

pin this together

side view

Sew along each line of pinched fabric.

Flip the shirt over. Fold it in half and mark the middle of the shirt back. Unfold the shirt and lay it flat on a work surface, back side facing up. Measure and mark 2 lines 4" outside of and parallel to the center line.

Mark every 2" along all 3 vertical lines. Cut the top layer of shirt along the center line, from the bottom to just below the collar.

Working from the center line to the left, make horizontal cuts at each 2" mark, stopping at the parallel line 4" away. Again, make sure to cut through only one piece of fabric. Repeat on right side of center line.

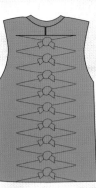

Turn the shirt right side out. Working from top to bottom, tie each set of strips into a square knot.

Try on the shirt to see how it fits, adjusting the knots if you need to. If the shirt is too small to tie the pieces together, sew them so that the undersides of the strips touch and the ends stick out.

While the shirt is on, mark how low you would like the neckline to be, and any adjustments you want to make to the sleeves. If the armholes are too big, pinch the bottoms of the holes together so the sleeves fit well and mark with pins. Take the shirt off and sew sleeves accordingly.

FREE
T-SHIRT
DAY

Take the shirt off and begin the neckline by cutting a straight vertical line down from the left shoulder, staying just inside the left seam strip and stopping when you reach the neckline mark. Make a horizontal cut straight across the front, stopping just before right seam strip. Cut a vertical line up to the right shoulder, the same distance from the right seam strip as on left side, and continue around the back.

To ensure that the sewn seam strips stay flat around the neckline, fold each strip on the inside of the shirt toward the outermost edge. Sew a few stitches at the shoulders to secure the strips in this position.

LITTLE IN THE MIDDLE

This very simple belt is great for adding a bit of color to a dress or shirt. Scrunch it up to make it look a bit thinner or spread it out for a much wider middle. Or add some bling with a large pin. The finished look is definitely all in the styling.

STEP 1

Team

Measure 10" up from the bottom of shirt and draw line parallel to the bottom edge. Cut shirt along this line.

STEP 2

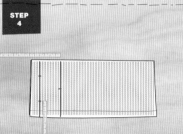

Cut one side seam (short side of rectangle) to create a long, 10"-wide strip. Wrap this strip around your waist. Find where the two pieces meet when pulled snugly around your waist (or your hips if you want your belt to rest there). Mark with tailor's chalk or a pin on each piece where it meets the other.

STEP 3

Fold strip inside out so marks made on each side of strip are touching. This creates a fold at what will be the center of belt. Draw a straight line down strip to indicate where each mark is. Next, make a small mark at the center of this line.

STEP 4

Draw a second line parallel to the first line and 4" closer to the cut ends of the strip. Measure and make a small mark 3" from top and bottom of this line.

STEP 5

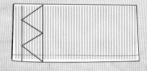

Draw a zigzag connecting the small marks you have made, starting at the top of the first (inner) line, tracing down to the first mark on the outer line and ending at the bottom of the inner line.

STEP 6

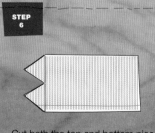

Cut both the top and bottom pieces of fabric together along zigzagged line.

STEP 7

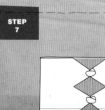

Put the belt around your waist and tie two small knots to join the triangular pieces at opposite ends.

Fit to Be Thai-d

work kit

- ◯ T-shirt for restyling
- ◯ Straight pins
- ◯ A shirt that fits you well
- ◯ Tailor's chalk or pencil (for marking)
- ◯ Needle and thread
- ◯ Scissors
- ◯ Straight-edge ruler

This style was inspired by a shirt my boyfriend Kevin brought me from Thailand. The strip in the back is one long piece, which I think is cool. The larger the T-shirt you start with, the more fabric you have to tie in back. If you don't want the loose strips hanging at the shoulders, tie the strips to each other for a different effect—or just cut them off entirely.

Fold the T-shirt for restyling in half to determine the center line. Mark with pins and iron if desired.

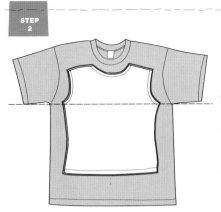

Align the underarms of the well-fitting shirt with the shirt to be restyled, and trace the outline with tailor's chalk or pencil.

Remove the top shirt and continue working on T-shirt to be restyled, pinning the front and back together. Sew the front and back of the T-shirt together along the newly marked shoulder lines. Do not sew across from one shoulder to the other, as you will need a neck opening.

Cut off the original shoulder seams from both sides of the shirt.

Mark 1" intervals along the top of original shoulder seams from neck to outer edge. Cut through both layers of fabric down to about 1/8" above new shoulders.

Cut and shape the neckline as desired (see ideas on page 12). Cut off the sleeves of the shirt, following the lines you traced. Starting at the underarm, sew shirt together along the side lines you marked. Make sure your stitches end at the bottom of marked shirt.

Starting under each arm and ending at the point where the new side seam ends, mark 1" segments down the side of the shirt. Cut the front and back of the shirt at the inch marks, from the outer seam to the sewn line, being careful not to cut into your new stitches. This will create loops at the side of the shirt. Repeat on the other side.

On the right-hand side, beneath the horizontal cuts and the side seam, make 1" marks down the original side of the shirt.

On the left-hand side, beneath the horizontal cuts and the side seam, make a mark that is only ½" down. Continuing from there, make 1" marks down the original side seam.

Draw diagonal lines to connect marks you just made. Cut a ¼" notch into side of shirt at each mark, cutting through both layers of fabric.

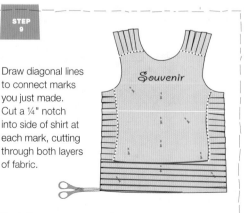

back

front

Flip the shirt over. Draw diagonal lines to connect the notches you just cut, making sure that the new lines match up with the lines already drawn on front of shirt. (These diagonal lines will slant in the same direction as the ones on the front.)

Remove pins from shirt bottom. Carefully cut fabric in one continuous line, following the spiral line you drew across first the front fabric, then the back fabric, and around again, until you have reached the new bottom edge of shirt. This will produce one long 1"-wide strip, hanging at one end from bottom of shirt.

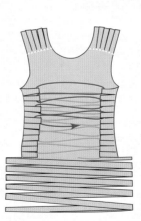

Lead the loose end of the strip in a zigzag across the shirt. Start at the bottom loop across from where the strip was attached, and weave it through every other loop on either side of the shirt. When you get to the top of the loops, weave the strip straight across to the other side and then down, zigzagging through the remaining empty loops.

Try on shirt and adjust width of zigzags to your size. When you are sure where to end the strip, pin, tie, or sew it into place so it does not come loose.

T-Bag

I like the way this bag shows off the T-shirt's graphic, reminding you of its former life. My friend Cindy made an awesome version of this bag using a white Amagansett T-shirt with bold navy letters across the front. She chose a contrasting red zipper and thread. The zipper can be a tad tricky to attach, but it isn't too hard and really makes the bag useful—so don't be scared off by it; just work slowly.

Cut off the hem from the bottom of the shirt, using the seam line as a guide and cutting through both layers of fabric at once. Cut the resulting loop once to create a strip of fabric. Cut the sleeves off the shirt using the seam line as a guide.

Cut along the shoulder seams from the arm to the neck on both sides.

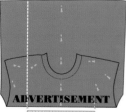

Reaching through the neck, pull the bottom end of the shirt up so that 8" of the shirt's top is still right side out while the rest of the shirt is inside out. Pin the shirt together this way. Find the vertical center of the shirt by folding it in half (armhole to armhole) and ironing or pinning the center line.

At the newly folded bottom edge, mark 6" on each side of the center point (12" total from left to right) with pins. Starting at the left-hand pin, using tailor's chalk or pencil, mark a line perpendicular to the shirt's new edge and extending up about 17", or all the way to the original bottom edge of the shirt. Sew along this perpendicular line.

STEP 5	STEP 6	STEP 7

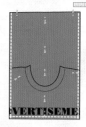

Cut the fabric to the left of perpendicular line, cutting about ⅛" outside of the sewn line and being very careful not to cut the stitches. If desired, use pinking shears for a decorative effect. Sew the marked 12" line along the folded bottom edge.

Fold the shirt down the center (as marked earlier), making sure that the center section lies on top of the folded fabric. Using the sewn edge as a guide, mark a new perpendicular line that, when the shirt is unfolded, will be 6" to the right of the center and at least 17" high.

Sew along this line and then cut away any excess fabric to the right of line, as you did with the left side. Along the top (unsewn) part of the resulting rectangle, measure and mark 1" in from the end of the stitches. This will be the width of your strap.

STEP 8	STEP 9	STEP 10

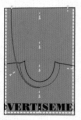

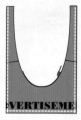

Using tailor's chalk, pencil, or pins, mark a scoop from the point just made to the bottom edge of the original shirt's neckline, stopping at the piece's center line. Cut along this second line until you reach the center point. (You may want to use pinking shears here as well.)

Fold the cut portion in half and use as a guide to mark the other side. Make sure to align the long sides, with the top of each scoop starting 1" away from the edge. Cut out the rest of the scoop.

Take out the pins from the bottom edge so you can open the bag. Center the zipper at bottom of the scoop and on the inside of the bag. There should be two layers of fabric on either side of zipper edge.

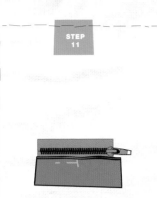

Pin one edge of the zipper to inner edge of bag, keeping zipper fabric on inside of bag and pinning both layers of fabric on that side. Make sure the zipper curves evenly with the line of the scoop.

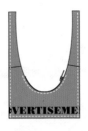

Sew one side of the zipper to the T-shirt layers it is pinned to. (This is easier to do by hand than with a sewing machine.)

Keeping the zipper closed, pin the other side of the zipper to the other side of the pouch, making sure the zipper edge stays inside the bag and is pinned to both layers of fabric. Also make sure that both sides of the zipper are aligned. Open the zipper. Sew the pinned side of the zipper to the bag.

Close the zipper once more and sew along the left inside edge of the scoop, from the top down to the start of the zipper's teeth. Be sure to tuck the excess material of the zipper inside the pouch as you sew the bag together.

Repeat on right inside edge of the scoop.

about 1½"

Sew strap together, beginning along outer edge of upper strap and continuing at right angles along side of strip, the outer edge of the lower strip, and remaining side, creating a square with your stitches. When you come back to the original corner, continue sewing in a diagonal across square before securing your thread with a knot.

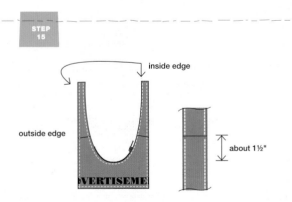

inside edge

outside edge

about 1½"

Hold the bag by the narrow ends. Before joining ends into one continuous strap, rotate one end so that the inside edge of that strip is aligned with the OUTSIDE edge of the other strip. This will add a twist to the shoulder strap. Overlap the ends by about 1½" and pin together.

i-Shirt

work kit

- ○ T-shirt for restyling
- ○ iPod or MP3 player
- ○ Straight-edge ruler
- ○ Tailor's chalk or pencil (for marking)
- ○ Scissors
- ○ Piece of paper or photocopy of the front of your player
- ○ Pen or pencil
- ○ Straight pins
- ○ Needle and thick thread

This cute little cover adds personality to your iPod or MP3 player. I like capturing a part of a T-shirt's graphic on it. Since width and design of iPod and MP3 players are different, I've written these instructions so they can be adapted to either.

Measure the height of your player and add 1". Mark and cut a horizontal strip to that height from your T-shirt, capturing the graphic if you like. Make sure the strip is long enough to wrap around your player at least once.

Good Cause

Copy the face of your player onto a piece of paper by measuring the face and drawing a window and a touch circle. (To make this step fast and easy, you can either place the paper on top of the player and carefully trace its face or photocopy it.)

With a pen or pencil, draw a line ⅛" in from the outer border of the player. Cut along this line so that your piece of paper is smaller than the face of your player, being careful not to cut too close to the window and touch areas. Cut a small hole into the center of the screen and touch circle areas.

If the touch pad and window are both centered across your player's front, place the paper face up (with drawn lines visible) on the wrong side of the strip of fabric. If the touch pad and window are not centered on your player's front, you will need to reverse the lines on the front of your paper by tracing them onto the back. You may want to hold the paper up to a sunny window to see the lines clearly. Place your paper on the wrong side of the strip of fabric, with the newly-traced (reversed) lines face up. Pin the paper in place.

Stitch the paper to the T-shirt around the window and touch pad frames. Starting at the small holes you cut in the center of the window and touch pad areas, carefully cut the paper away from these areas, staying inside the stitches.

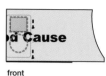

front

Carefully cut the T-shirt fabric away from the window area. Test whether the touch pad works on your player through the T-shirt fabric. If so, leave the fabric in place. If not, carefully cut the fabric away from the touch pad area as well, staying inside the stitches.

Position the window you have just cut over the window of your player, so the paper touches the face of your player and the fabric is right side up. Wrap the T-shirt around the player and pin it tightly on one side.

STEP
8

Sew this pinned side, beginning at the top of the player. When you reach the bottom of the side, continue to sew around the corner up to the charger hole. Secure your thread with a knot. Sew the remaining part of the bottom edge, beginning on the other side of the charger hole. Cut off the excess material around the player.

COASTERS 'N' PLACEMATS

I love the idea of setting the table with these coasters and placemats, especially the ones made from T-shirts with interesting graphics and pockets—it's such a fun way to mix high and low style.

Placemat (Coaster)

STEP 1
Lay the shirt down flat. Using a ruler and tailor's chalk or pencil, measure and mark a rectangle for placemat (square for coaster) that is about 18" x 14" (4"x4").

STEP 2
Pin the top and bottom fabric together or, for a tighter hold, apply a small amount of fabric glue.

STEP 3
Cut out the rectangle (square). If you want a fancy edge, use pinking shears.

STEP 4
Sew along the perimeter to finish.

ACKNOWLEDGMENTS

Thank you, Melanie Falick! It may be too obvious to say, but there is a reason you have your own imprint. You are one smart, hardworking gal! Once again, thanks for your enthusiasm for my work and your dedication to perfecting each project. Vanessa Gifford, thank you for actually dumping a (mini) sewing machine upon me—you were right, it was fast and easy. Thanks to Julie Sandy for helping with a collar. **Thank you, Cindy Forrest, for all of your hard work following my instructions and helping to complete the samples for the photo shoot. Yours were often better than my own.** *Either I'm one smooth talker or (more likely) Cristin Houlihan is one of the best friends anyone could have. She came all the way from Boston to my apartment/sweatshop in New York City to help me prepare for the photo shoot.* **Wow. Thanks.** Sarah Von Dreele—I love that you are so prepared for every meeting and that you have been so involved with this project from day one. Your talent and vision seem to match perfectly with my own, which comes as a wonderful relief to me. **Adrian Buckmaster and crew (Kristin, Ali, and Terry), it was awesome to work with such a talented, professional, and fun team. The shoot was both a pleasure and a success. Thank you so much to the models who lent me their days and/or afternoons: Alexandra Levin, Todd Coleman, Nami Payackapan, Kevin Lertkhachonsuk, Gwyn Wells, Nathan Garber, Kodos (the dog), and Amanda Barlow.** Thanks to Larry Oraa and Frances Lachowitz for providing me with graphics for the sample T-shirt. **Robie and Fred Rogge (the 'rents), thank you very much for your enthusiasm, excitement, and mostly for helping me in every way that you can. I couldn't have accomplished what I have over the past year without you. (Also, thanks for putting up with my crankiness and fatigue.)** Brian Healy, you did a great job with the venue for the first book party—you're on for the next.

And Kevin, ah, well, you made it to the dedication page for a reason.

Hannah Rogge, a graduate of the Rhode Island School of Design, works in New York City designing and building exhibits, visual merchandising displays, and animated windows. She is the author of *Hardwear: Jewelry from a Toolbox* (Stewart, Tabori & Chang, 2006).